FORTUNE-TELLING
BOOK OF NAMES

This book belongs to

_____

The gift of

_____

A. M. McCloud
Illustrations by Jennifer Sly

CHRONICLE BOOKS
SAN FRANCISCO

HOW TO USE THIS BOOK

BEATRICE

Language of Origin   *Alternate Spellings*   *Nicknames*

(Latin) Beatrise, Beatrix; Bea, Bee, Trish, Trixie;
Beatriz (Spanish)

Fortune   *Name in other language(s)*

**You are blessed with good fortune. A period of tremendous joy
is on the horizon. Share it with others, and you will reap an
even greater reward.**

Note: Categories (Alternate Spellings, Nicknames, and
Name in other language(s)) are separated by semicolons.

GIRL NAMES

AALIYAH

(Hebrew)

In the lobby of a nondescript hotel, in a remote town, you will meet your true love.

ABIGAIL

(Hebrew) Abagail, Abbigail, Abigale, Abigayle; Abbey, Abbie, Abby, Gail, Gayle

You will take great joy from the simplest of pleasures.

ADDISON

(English) Addyson; Addie, Addy

Your awe-inspiring focus and attention to detail will bring you tremendous success in your career.

ADRIENNE

(Latin, Greek) Adriane, Adrian, Adrianne

There are vast wealth and material possessions in your future.

AGNES

(Greek) Aggie, Aggy

You are pure of heart and mind.

ALEXANDRA

(Greek) Alexandre, Alexandria; Alex, Alexa, Alexis, Lex, Lexi, Lexie; Alejandra (Spanish)

You will earn the respect and admiration of your community through tireless altruism.

ALICE

(Greek), Alicia (English), Alize (German)

Honesty and sincerity will bring you much success in your endeavors.

ALIN

(Scottish)

A trip into your past will help you better appreciate your present.

ALLISON

(English) Alison, Allyson

Your benevolence will be greatly appreciated, but beware of those who may try to take advantage of it.

ALYSSA

(Greek) Alissa

Use your beauty wisely, or it will become more of a curse than a blessing.

AMANDA

(Latin) Manda, Mandi, Mandy

Be patient. You are fated for true love.

AMBER

(French)

Money matters are your forte. Matters of the heart, however, are another story. Not everything can be calculated.

AMELIA

(German)

You will be rewarded financially and professionally for your diligence and industriousness.

AMY

(Latin) Aimee, Amie, Ami

Friends and family love and adore you. Domestic bliss is in your future.

ANDREA

(Greek) Andi, Andie, Andy

You are strong and feminine, a most fortunate pairing. Success is limitless.

ANGELA

(Greek)

A risky endeavor will be wildly successful.

ANGELINA

(Latin) Angeline; Angie

Your angelic demeanor and generosity of spirit make you a source of inspiration. You will use your influence to guide those who are lost.

ANN

(Hebrew) Anne; Annie

Your propensity to love is a beautiful but dangerous
thing. Be careful with your heart.

ANNA

(Hebrew)

Gather your strength. You're going to need it.

ANNABELLE

(English) Annabel

Your benevolence will not go unrewarded.

ANSLEY

(English) Ainsley, Ainslie

You will find joy and success in a profession that involves
the outdoors.

ARABELLA

(Latin)

A good friendship will lay the groundwork for a lasting
love affair.

ARDEN

(Latin)

Unexpected travel will reveal a unique opportunity.

ARIANA

(Greek) Arianna

There's nothing to fear. Marriage and motherhood will suit you.

ARLENE

(Irish) Arleen; Lena, Lina

Through discipline and dedication, a goal you thought unattainable will be realized.

ASHLEY

(English) Ashlee, Ashleigh, Ashly; Lee, Leigh

Your playful spirit will lead you into questionable situations. Use discretion, or you may find yourself in hot water.

ASHLYN

(English) Ashlan, Ashlynn

Your dreamlike vision of the future will only come to fruition through decisive action. Take charge!

AUBREY

(German)

The clouds are about to part. Happy times with friends and family lie ahead.

AUDREY

(English)

Motherhood will come early to you. Look to friends and family for help.

AUTUMN

(Latin)

Your energetic nature and creative mind will bring you
tremendous career success.

AVA

(Latin)

Delicate handling of problematic people will help you
advance your career.

AVERY

(English)

Flirtatious behavior will get you into trouble. Make sure
your intentions are clear.

BOY NAMES

AARON

(Hebrew) Aaren, Aarin, Aaryn, Aron

You will be revered for your business acumen.

ABRAHAM

(Hebrew) Aberham, Abhiram, Abram; Abe, Bram

You will father many children.

ADAM

(Hebrew)

Your originality will be a source of much success in personal and professional affairs.

ADRIAN

(Latin) Adarian, Adreian, Adriann, Adrien, Adryan

Money will never be a concern for you. Your pockets will be forever full.

AIDAN

(Irish) Aiden, Aydan, Ayden, Aydin

Don't allow passion to hamper your otherwise good judgment, or your reputation will suffer.

ALAN

(Irish) Al, Alen, Allan, Allen

Your seemingly endless charm and natty appearance will win many hearts.

ALBERT

(German) Alberte, Elbert, Al, Albie

You will distinguish yourself at work. Anticipate a promotion.

ALCOTT

(English) Alcot, Allcot, Allcott

Your great appreciation of leisure does not bode well for your professional endeavors.

ALDEN

(English)

You will find yourself in a situation where great wisdom and courage are necessary. Your leadership will be admired.

ALEXANDER

(Greek) Alexandar, Alexsander; Alec, Alex, Zander, Xander; Alejandro (Spanish)

You will take the lead on a project. Be careful not to alienate your underlings, or your success will be hampered.

ALFRED

(English) Alfrede, Alfryd; Alf, Alfie, Fred; Alfredo (Spanish)

A friend will seek your counsel. Your opinion will change his course for the better.

AMES

(French)

You will have many good friends and enjoy frequent social gatherings.

ANDREW

(Greek) Andrews; Andie, Andy, Drew; Anders (Swedish), Andres (Spanish)

Don't let courage turn into bravado, or your professional relationships will sour.

ANSEL

(French) Ansyl

Your creativity will eventually lead you to success.
Don't give up!

ANTHONY

(Latin) Anthoney, Anthoni, Antony; Tony; Antonio (Italian)

Someone will come to you for advice. Give it. Friends and
associates find your opinions invaluable.

ARCHER

(English) Archor; Archie

Your athletic prowess will be the source of great prosperity.

ARI

(Greek) Arie, Arih, Arri, Ary

You are destined to be the best at whatever you do.

ARNOLD

(German) Arnald; Arnie, Arny; Arnoldo (Spanish)

You will be asked to take the lead at work. Meet the
challenge, and you'll be handsomely rewarded.

ASHBY

(Scandinavian) Ashbee, Ashbey

Impetuous behavior will get you into trouble. Seriously
consider your decision on a pressing matter, or the result
with forever haunt you.

ASHTON

(English) Ashtan, Ashtyn

You will feel suffocated and will gravitate toward
openness and freedom.

AUSTIN

(Latin) Astin, Augustine, Austine, Auston

Your serious nature will win you success in your work life,
but your love life will suffer.

GIRL NAMES

BAILEY

(English) Bailee, Baylee

Decadence could get you into trouble. Mind your manners and you won't have any problems.

BARBARA

(Latin) Babs, Barb, Barbie

A good marriage will keep you healthy and happy.

BEATRICE

(Latin) Beatrise, Beatrix; Bea, Bee, Trish, Trixie; Beatriz (Spanish)

You are blessed with good fortune. A period of tremendous joy is on the horizon. Share it with others, and you will reap an even greater reward.

BELINDA

(Spanish) Blinda

Great beauty has been bestowed upon you. Exercise humility, or it will get in the way of an important relationship.

BELLA

(Italian)

You will be surrounded by luxury and will enjoy many hobbies.

BETHANY

(Hebrew)

A divinely inspired journey will forever change your life.

BEVERLY

(English) Beverley; Bev, Buffy

Your friendly nature will attract many people. Beware of those who try to take advantage of your generous spirit. Their loyalty is not true.

BIANCA

(Italian) Biancca, Bianka; Blanche (French)

Your beloved is pure of heart. Stop questioning his intentions.

BLAIR

(Scottish) Blaire

You battle your innate desire for solitude. This keeps you from true happiness. Don't force friendships. You're not the only one who suffers.

BLYTHE

(English) Blithe

Your carefree approach to life will get you into hot water at work. Meet your responsibilities, or suffer a setback.

BRADLEY

(English) Bradlee, Bradlie

A friend needs a dose of your optimism and humor.

BRANDY

(Dutch) Brandi

The fun-loving, sweet side of you will find the door to opportunity. The hardworking, diligent side of you will open it.

BRETT

(Latin) Bret, Brette

An indiscretion will be made public. But don't worry; the flurry of gossip will be fleeting.

BRIANNA

(Irish) Breana, Briana; Bria, Briah, Brea, Bree

Your virtuous nature will win hearts. Don't let the pressure of a suitor lead you astray.

BRIDGET

(Irish) Bridgett, Bridgette, Brigid; Gitta;
Birgitta (Scandinavian), Brigette (French), Bryga (Polish)

A strong will and fierce spirit is your blessing and curse. You will create obstacles for yourself if you don't allow for varying opinions.

BRITTANY

(English) Britaney, Britany, Britney

Your clever wit will captivate and intimidate. Use it wisely, and professional and personal success will be yours.

BROOKE

(English) Brook; Brookie, Brooky

A persistent problem requires a sophisticated solution.
It's in you. Just look.

BROOKLYN

(American) Brooklin

Your tough exterior overshadows a sensitive nature. Your
obstacles will not be easily subdued unless you strike a
balance between the two.

BRYCE

(Welsh) Brice

A keen social awareness will bring you success at home
and at work.

BRYN

(Welsh) Brin, Brinn, Brynn, Brynne

You have your feet in two worlds, and this causes you
great anxiety. Simply open the door between them, and
your worries are over.

BOY NAMES

BARAK

(Hebrew) Barrak, Barack

Only through courage and determination will you overcome a debilitating obstacle.

BARRETT

(German) Baret, Barett

You will shoulder a large burden. Look to others to help lessen the weight.

BENJAMIN

(Hebrew) Benjamen, Benjiman; Ben, Bennie, Benny, Benji

You will stand in someone's shadow for too long. Step into the light and shine.

BENNETT

(French) Benet, Benett, Benette

Financial endeavors are blessed with good luck. Anticipate success.

BENSON

(Hebrew) Bensan, Bensen

You will become involved in a situation that could cause you embarrassment unless discretion is exercised.

BLAKE

(English) Blaike, Blayke

A romantic liaison is in your future. Don't let passion
overcome reason, or you're in trouble.

BODIE

(Scandinavian) Bodey, Bodi; Bodhi (Chinese)

Your relaxed approach to a current problem does little to
move you closer to a resolution. Unless thought and energy
are put into the solution, you will be very unhappy with
the result.

BOOKER

(English)

Your worries are for naught. You are overthinking a
problem. Simply see it for what it is, and you will be freed
from its grasp.

BOOTH

(English) Boothe

A friend will often look to you for protection. He will never
learn to fight for himself if you're always there to fight
for him. Let him defend himself. You will both reap a
positive result.

BOYD

(Scottish) Boid, Boyde

A beautiful blond stranger will come into your life.
Resist her charms if you can.

BRADLEY

(English) Bradlee, Bradlie, Bradly; Brad

**The gods of money and wealth shine upon you.
Great prosperity is in your future.**

BRANDON

(English) Brandan, Brandonn

**You will be faced with an important decision. You'll know
the answer but will feel threatened by the repercussions.
Do what you know is right, and there is nothing to fear.**

BRANDT

(English) Brant

**The dignified handling of a complicated situation will
win you advocates and admirers.**

BRAYDEN

(English) Braydan, Braydon

Your efficiency will bring you great financial success.

BRENDAN

(Irish) Brenden, Brendon

**You are long on ideas and short on action. Balance the
two, and you will find success.**

BRENT

(English) Brendt, Brente

Exhaustive preparation will help you reach your goal.

BRIAN

(Irish) Brien, Bryan; Bri, Bry

You will be publicly recognized for an honorable action.

BRODY

(Irish) Brodee, Brodie

Hard work and sustained effort will award you a modest but happy life.

BROOKS

(English) Brookes

Your easygoing approach to your finances will usher in the creditors. Learn how to manage your money, or you will forever be in debt.

BRUCE

(French)

Someone is resisting change. Be persistent, and he will change his tune.

BYRON

(English) Byren, Byrone

Unexpected social pleasures are in store for you.

GIRL NAMES

CAITLIN

(Irish) Caitlan, Caitlen, Caitlyn, Kaitlin, Kaitlyn, Katelyn

You will be rewarded for the care and attention you pay to
those in need.

CAMERON

(Scottish) Camren, Camryn

Your popularity will soar. Anticipate a sudden rise in
social status.

CARLY

(English) Carlee, Carley, Carlie, Karley

A long-awaited event will be postponed. But don't worry, it
will happen, and when it does, it will far exceed
your expectations.

CARMEN

(Latin) Carman, Carmon

You will have a successful career in the arts,
particularly music.

CAROLINE

(Latin) Carolyn; Carrie

You underestimate yourself. You've got a solid head on your
shoulders. Use it.

CASEY

(Irish) Kasey

You will have to weather a particularly sticky situation but will come out of it on top.

CATHERINE

(Greek) Katherine; Cat, Cate, Kate, Kathy, Katie, Kitty

A gift you have forever coveted will be bestowed upon you by a close friend.

CHARLOTTE

(French) Charlette, Charlott; Tottie

Your community will honor you for your altruism.

CHELSEA

(English) Chelsee, Chelsey

A current goal will be easily realized. Set your sights higher. The world is your oyster.

CHLOE

(Greek) Chloey

Your vibrancy and enthusiasm will bring you monetary success.

CHRISTINA

(Greek) Christiana, Kristina;
Chris, Chrissie, Christie, Christy, Kris, Tina

Your spirituality, whatever form it takes, will lead you to personal fulfillment.

CHRISTINE

(French)

A casual romance will evolve into a lifelong love affair.

CLAIRE

(French) Clair, Clare

The stars shine brightly on you. What you perceive as bad luck is opportunity in disguise.

CLARISSA

(Greek) Clarisa

Your intelligence will bring you career success but difficulties in love. There is a time to follow the mind and a time to follow the heart.

CLAUDIA

(Latin) Claude

You will fall in love with a famous theatrical performer.

COLBY

(English) Colbee, Colbey

Think endurance. You will move beyond a debilitating obstacle only if you have the patience to work through it.

COLETTE

(French) Collette; Cole

Victory is at hand! You will triumph over a professional adversary.

COLLEEN

(Irish) Coleen, Colleene

Your youthful approach to life will bring you great
personal happiness.

CONSTANCE

(Latin) Connie; Constanza (Spanish)

Blind devotion will bring you trouble. Remember, loyalty
is owed only to those who earn it.

COURTNEY

(English) Courtenay, Courteney, Courtny

You will be personally and professionally rewarded for
your reliability.

CYNTHIA

(Greek)

Your mercurial nature might frustrate those around you.

BOY NAMES

CADEN

(English) Cadan, Caiden, Kaden, Kaiden, Kayden

You will have a spirited exchange with a stranger that will lead to employment.

CALEB

(Hebrew) Calab, Kaleb, Kayleb

You overexert and overextend yourself. Success will be yours if you just focus your energy.

CAMERON

(Scottish) Cameren, Kameron

Mischievous behavior will get you into hot water. A bouquet of flowers should sort things out.

CARLOS

(Spanish)

Machismo is not the answer to your problems. Reevaluate your approach.

CARSON

(English) Carsen

Hard work and confidence in your abilities will win you a promotion.

CARTER

(English) Cartar

You will make a discovery that brings you fame and fortune.

CASSIDY

(Irish) Casidy, Cassady; Cass

You are destined for a career in comedy.

CHARLES

(German) Chad, Charlie, Chaz, Chuck

An adoring family and a close circle of good friends are in your future.

CHASE

(French) Chayse

You are hunting for an answer that is right under your nose.

CHRISTIAN

(Latin) Christen, Cristian; Chris

An adventure to a foreign land will bring you closer to someone you thought forever lost.

CHRISTOPHER

(Greek) Christofer, Christoffer, Cristopher; Chris, Topher

Someone is trying to undermine you. Beware of treachery.

CLIFFORD

(English) Cliford, Clyford; Cliff

You will take a sizable risk that will bring minimal return.
Use your resources wisely, or you will suffer.

CLIVE

(English) Clyve

Your daring will win you many hearts.

CODY

(English) Coady, Codie

You are destined for a modest but comfortable life.

COLE

(Greek)

You will win a risky bet and will gain something valuable—
maybe money, maybe a lover, maybe experience.

COLIN

(Irish), Collin (Scottish)

You will receive news that will bring much-needed peace
of mind.

COLTON

(English) Colten

You will achieve success you once thought impossible.

CONNOR

(Scottish) Conner

An elaborate celebration of your accomplishments is in
your near future.

COOPER

(English) Couper; Coop

Hard work and discipline will bring a dramatic increase
in income.

CRAIG

(Irish)

You will be asked to account for an indiscretion you
thought long-forgotten.

CULLEN

(Irish) Cullan, Cullin, Culyn

An unexpected love affair will forever change your life.

CURTIS

(French) Curtice, Kurtis; Curt, Kurt

Your kindness and generosity will leave you overextended.
Be careful, or the creditors will come calling.

GIRL NAMES

DAHLIA

(Scandinavian) Dahliah, Dalia

Good news regarding your financial situation is on the way.

DAISY

(English)

Your impulsivity will get you into hot water, particularly in your investment decisions.

DANA

(English)

Anticipate interesting new friends and fun social gatherings in the near future.

DANIELLE

(Hebrew) Danni, Danny

Success in a difficult endeavor is yours but only after a period of frustration.

DAPHNE

(Greek) Daphney, Daphnie

You will learn a secret you'd rather not. Keep it to yourself, and it will do no harm.

DARCY

(Irish) Darci, Darcie

A brief period of stormy weather is on the horizon. Batten down the hatches.

DARLA

(English)

Beware: Someone is masquerading as a friend.

DARREN

(Irish) Darrin, Daryn

You are in line for a season of great success. Take advantage of it!

DARRYL

(French) Darrell, Daryl

Some form of profit is en route, though possibly not as hefty as you'd hoped.

DASHA

(Russian)

Your current goal will not be attained as easily as anticipated. Buckle down, and you'll get there.

DEBORAH

(Hebrew) Debra; Deb, Debbie

A surprise will bring an advantageous change in circumstance.

DEIRDRE

(Irish) Deidre

A rare opportunity will present itself to you. Grab it, and you won't be sorry.

DELILAH

(Hebrew)

An impulsive romantic liaison will turn into a lifelong love affair.

DENI

(English)

You must maneuver around obstacles and adversaries to reach your goal.

DENISE

(French)

You are prepared to take a big risk but are afraid of the consequences. Don't be. All signs point to success.

DESTINY

(French) Destinee, Destiney, Destini

A small change in your life will have a huge effect on your future.

DEVIN

(Irish) Devon, Devyn

The success of a creative endeavor will set a promising tone for the future.

DIANA

(Latin) Dianna; Di, Didi

A crisis will arise, and family and friends will turn to you to take control.

DOMINIQUE

(French)

Slow down. Overindulgence will get you into trouble.

DONNA

(Italian)

All of your sacrificing and selflessness will be well worth it. You'll see.

DORA

(Greek)

The realization of a short-term goal will set you up for even greater success.

DOROTHY

(Greek) Dottie

You will profit from a wise investment.

DORSEY

(French)

You will be unexpectedly recognized and honored for past good deeds.

DREW

(Greek)

Remember, even true love has blemishes. So he's not perfect. Nobody is.

BOY NAMES

DALE

(English) Dail, Dayle

Your efforts are not made in vain. You will see surprisingly high returns in a short period of time.

DAMIAN

(Greek) Damien, Damion

You will marry a woman of ample means.

DANE

(English) Dain, Dayne

News that will necessitate international travel will arrive by mail. Pack your bags!

DANIEL

(Hebrew) Danial, Danniel; Dan, Dannie, Danny

You will take a spiritual pilgrimage that will bring you tremendous peace.

DARREN

(Irish) Daren, Darin, Darrin

Greatness is in your future. You are headed in the right direction regardless of what others say. Stay the course!

DAVID

(Hebrew) Dave, Davey, Davy

Keep your heart and mind open. True love is before you if you'd only see it.

DAVIS

(Welsh)

Ambition is blinding you. Slow down and open your eyes, or you'll miss what's really important.

DAWSON

(English) Dawsan, Dawsen

A surprising romance will drastically change your course for the better. Don't fight it.

DAX

(French)

Your unique approach to problem-solving will earn you a promotion at work.

DEAN

(English) Deane, Deen

A born leader, you are always ahead of the curve. Skeptics will question your decisions and will try to undermine your confidence. Ignore them. You are fated for success.

DENNIS

(Greek) Denny

You love the finer things in life, but beware of
overindulgence or you could suffer a setback.

DENTON

(English) Dentan, Denten

You are destined for domestic bliss. A happy and
contented family will carry you into old age.

DEREK

(German) Derrick; Dirk

After much deliberation, you'll take a major career risk.
Don't worry, it will prove to be a wise decision.
Tremendous financial success is in your future.

DEVIN

(Irish) Devon; Dev

Be it writing, painting, or sculpting, you are fated for a
career in the arts.

DIEGO

(Spanish)

Your magnetic personality will bring you much personal
and professional success.

DIGBY

(Irish) Digbe, Digbie

You will live a simple but happy life.

DIXON

(English) Dixen; Dix

A seemingly bad decision will eventually bring you great joy.

DOMINIC

(Latin) Dom; Domenico (Italian), Dominique (French)

Your faith in someone is misguided. His intentions are not as pure as they seem.

DOUGLAS

(Scottish) Douglass; Doug

A dark period is in your forecast. Face the challenges with strength and courage, and you will eventually overcome them.

DYLAN

(Welsh) Dillon

Someone will try to dissuade you from embarking on a creative endeavor. Disregard the advice; you're onto something.

GIRL NAMES

ELEANOR

(French) Ellie, Nellie, Lena, Nora; Eleanora (Greek)

You will make an advantageous contact at a social event.

ELENA

(Spanish)

Great career success is fated for you.

ELIZABETH

(Hebrew) Elisabeth, Lizbeth; Beth, Betsy, Betty, Buffy, Elise, Eliza, Elsa, Libby, Liz, Lizzie, Liza

You need never worry about money.

ELLA

(German)

Your imagination and creativity will land you a job in the arts.

ELLE

(French)

You will marry a man who appreciates your beauty as well as your intellect.

ELLEN

(English)

You will travel to many foreign lands for work and pleasure.

EMILY

(Latin), Emilia (Italian, Spanish), Émilie (French), Emelie (German)

Don't turn your back on a mysterious stranger. He will bring you good luck.

EMMA

(German)

You will finally receive money that is long overdue.

EMMY

(German) Emme, Emmi

An unusual situation will force you to better use your resources.

ERICA

(Norse) Ericka, Erika

You will be wooed by a wealthy suitor. He may have more money than integrity, however.

ERIN

(Irish) Erinn, Eryn

An investment will earn rich returns.

ESMÉ

(French)

You will go on a grand adventure with a new lover.

ESTELLE

(French)

You shine brighter than most. This will win you popularity and professional success.

ESTHER

(Persian) Ester, Eszter; Estée (French)

The night sky will guide you away from a dangerous situation.

ETANA

(Hebrew)

Your strength of purpose will bring you tremendous career success.

ETTA

(English)

A goal you once thought completely out of reach will become attainable.

EVA

(Hebrew)

Good health and vitality will be yours throughout life.

EVANA

(Greek)

The coming year will bring you much happiness.

EVANGELINE

(Greek)

You will have a good marriage that will bring you great joy.

EVELYN

(English) Evelin

A new love interest will soon move to town.

BOY NAMES

EATON

(English) Eton, Eyton

You are fated for wealth and all of its trappings.

EDGAR

(English)

A challenging endeavor will be a tremendous success and will set the wheels in motion for a promotion.

EDMUND

(English) Edmon, Edmond

Your overprotective tendencies will cause you problems in a romantic relationship.

EDWARD

(English) Ed, Eddie, Ned, Ted, Teddy

Through focused effort and dedication, you will have great prosperity.

EGAN

(Irish) Egann, Egyn

You will finally make a decision that has kept you from moving forward. The decision is a good one and will set the stage for future success.

ELAN

(Hebrew) Elon, Ilan

An unforeseen trip is in your future. You will reunite with an old friend, and this reunion will prove to be personally and professionally advantageous.

ELI

(Hebrew) Ely

Your unyielding faithfulness and loyalty to friends and family will bring you domestic bliss and satisfaction.

ELIAS

(Greek) Elyas

Indifference makes you professionally stagnant. When your passion is finally ignited, positive change will follow.

ELIJAH

(Hebrew) Elija

Your instincts are right. A risky investment will pay off.

ELLIOTT

(English) Eliot, Elliot

You will divulge a secret that will forever change your life. What type of change depends on how you navigate the situation.

ELLISON

(English) Ellisen, Ellyson

A cautious approach is not always the best approach. Don't be afraid to take a chance, or opportunity will pass you by.

ELLSWORTH

(English) Elsworth

Misfortune will haunt you unless you meet the expectations you set for yourself.

EMILIO

(Italian)

You will battle fierce competition on the road to success, and there will be days filled with doubt. But know in the end, the fight is yours!

EMMANUEL

(Hebrew) Emanuel; Mannie, Manny

A beautiful but unscrupulous woman will distract you from what's truly important. Don't lose your head, or you will also lose your fortune.

EMMETT

(English) Emmitt

You will take great pleasure in the company of new, interesting friends.

ERIC

(Scandinavian) Erick, Erik

A secure, peaceful future lies ahead for you.

ERNESTO

(Spanish)

A period of unrest is at hand. Eliminate the negative forces at work, and it will be short-lived.

ETHAN

(Hebrew) Ethen

You will successfully negotiate an important deal that will bring you much monetary gain.

EVAN

(Irish) Evon

Don't be frustrated by career misfortune. Something bigger and better awaits.

EVERETT

(English) Everet, Everitt

Your quiet progress will lead to a tremendous achievement for which you will be honored publicly.

GIRL NAMES

FAITH

(English) Fayth; Fay, Faye

Many impressive academic achievements are predicted for you.

FAUSTINE

(Italian)

Lucky you! Your life and endeavors are forever blessed with good fortune.

FEDERICA

(Italian), Frederica (German)

You will rule your workplace with a strong but benevolent hand.

FELICIA

(Latin)

A most auspicious name. Good things will come to you.

FELICITY

(Latin)

You will find happiness and take great pride in your chosen career.

FINLEY

(Irish)

Hang in there. A positive change of fortune is foretold.

FIONA

(Scottish) Fee

You will have a happy home and loving children.

FLANNERY

(Irish) Flanery

A difficult journey will challenge but ultimately
reward you.

FLOR

(Spanish)

Great prosperity is foreseen for you.

FLORA

(Latin)

A troubling family situation will have a surprisingly
positive resolution.

FRANCES

(Latin) Francis; Fanny, Fran, Frankie, Frannie, Franny;
Francesca (Italian)

A season of great success is in store for you. Now is the
time to take risks.

FREDA

(German) Frieda, Frida

Chin up. The sad end to a trying love affair will bring
much-needed relief and clarity.

BOY NAMES

FAGIN

(Irish) Fagan

Your temper will get you into trouble. Learn to channel your anger, or suffer repeated setbacks.

FANE

(English) Fain, Faine, Fayne

Anticipate happy tidings from a friend whom you have not seen in years.

FELIX

(Latin); Felicio (Spanish), Feliks (Russian)

Extended international travel is in your future. You will spend a great deal of time away from home.

FENTON

(English) Fen, Fenn

A career in the outdoors is fated for you.

FERGUSON

(Irish)

A series of unfortunate events are in store for you. Weather these misfortunes with dignity and grace, and you will be rewarded.

FERNANDO

(Spanish)

A rare opportunity will come knocking. Embrace it.

FERRIS

(Irish) Farris

An unexpected love affair will bring you great joy.

FIELDING

(English)

You are due for a long period of financial stress.
Avoid risk and use your resources wisely, and you'll
get through it.

FINN

(Irish) Fynn

A slight indiscretion will temporarily get you into trouble, but
your good humor will help you weather the storm.

FINNEGAN

(Irish) Finnigan

You will be faced with an obstacle that seems insurmount-
able. Don't give up. If taken day by day, it can be overcome.

FISHER

(English) Fischer

Someone in your circle is on the take. Be careful whom
you trust.

FLEMING

(English) Flemming

You will meet a famous performer with whom you will form a lifelong bond.

FLETCHER

(English) Fletch

You will be asked to account for some questionable behavior. Tell the truth, and you're in the clear. Dishonesty will only get you into more trouble.

FLYNN

(Irish) Flinn, Flyn

Something unexpected and unusual will occur that will cause you great pleasure and satisfaction.

FORD

(English) Forde

Your jealously will cause an unpleasant situation. Be careful, or a relationship will be severed.

FORESTER

(English) Forrester; Foster

You will take a calculated risk that will pay off handsomely. Invest the return wisely, and you'll be set for life.

FRANCIS

(Latin) Fran; François (French), Francisco (Spanish), Frantz (German)

A carefree attitude will create problems in your personal and professional life. Take something seriously, or success will be forever out of reach.

FRANKLIN

(English) Franklyn; Frank, Frankie

You will make a decision that will change your surroundings for the better.

FRASER

(French) Frasier, Frazer, Frazier

A change in career will cause you a temporary setback. Stay with it, and your future will be secure.

FREDERICK

(German) Frederic, Fredrick; Fred, Freddie, Freddy, Fritz, Fritzie; Federico (Spanish), Rico; Frédéric (French)

Repeating confidences will get you into hot water with a friend. Shush!

GIRL NAMES

GABRIELLA

(Italian/Spanish) Gabriela; Gabbie, Gabby, Gabi, Gaby, Gigi

You look back on unhappy times with regret. Look forward instead; happy times await.

GABRIELLE

(French)

Glamour and good fortune are destined for you.

GALEN

(Greek) Gaelen, Gaylen

Your unique and creative approach to business will bring you great personal satisfaction and professional success.

GARNET

(English)

Women in your circle will try to persuade you, but be sure to chart your own course.

GEORGETTE

(French) Georgie

Extravagant living will tax your budget. Be careful, or the champagne will soon run dry.

GEORGIA

(Greek)

A romantic entanglement will raise eyebrows.
Who cares? Have fun!

GIANNA

(Italian) Giana

You will experience a success when you expected
a failure.

GILLIAN

(Latin) Jillian

You will be a guest at an influential political gathering.

GINA

(Italian) Geena

Others muddle your thinking. You can solve a pressing
problem on your own.

GISELLE

(German) Gisele, Gisselle

You will be extremely popular with men.

GLORIA

(Latin)

Disappointment in love will be eclipsed by
career success.

GRACE

(Latin) Gracie

An unexpected experience will open your eyes to a new way of thinking.

GREER

(Scottish) Grier

Your intensity and enthusiasm will win hearts and minds.

GRETA

(German)

A heated argument with a friend will expose the long-buried truth. Use it to help solve the problem, not escalate it.

GRETCHEN

(German)

Careless statements and accusations will get you into hot water. Use your words wisely.

GWENDOLYN

(Welsh) Gwendolen; Gwen

You will be honored for a professional achievement.

GWYNETH

(Welsh)

True happiness is fated for you.

BOY NAMES

GABRIEL

(Hebrew) Gabrielle, Gabryel; Gabby, Gabe; Gabriele (Italian)

Your devotion to a project will bring you unimagined success.

GARETH

(Welsh) Garreth

You will have a career in politics, though it may be short-lived.

GARRETT

(Irish) Garret

Your passion for another will be unrequited. But chin up; love will find you again.

GARRISON

(English)

You pine for a past that is long gone. Look to the future, and you will find a solution to your problems.

GARTH

(Scandinavian) Garthe

The sun shines on an important endeavor. Happy times are ahead.

GARY

(English) Gari, Garrie, Garry

Don't harbor a grudge over a past wrong, or risk losing a
friend forever.

GAVIN

(Celtic) Gaven, Gavyn; Gavino (Italian)

Something will happen to make you question your course
of action. This is good. Revisions to your original plan are
necessary for success.

GEORGE

(Greek) Georgie; Georges (French), Georgio (Italian),
Jorge (Spanish)

Greater responsibilities will be added to your current role at
work. Face the new challenges enthusiastically, and you will
be rewarded.

GERARD

(English) Gerrard; Gerardo (Italian), Gerhard (German),
Jerardo (Spanish)

You will be very successful in your profession, but you will
work very hard for that success.

GIBSON

(English) Gibbson; Gibb

A romantic relationship will force you to reevaluate
your priorities.

GLENN

(Scottish) Glen, Glynn

Wedge yourself from a rut, or you may be permanently stuck there.

GORDON

(Scottish) Gordie, Gordy

A heated love affair will turn ugly if you are not honest about your intentions.

GRANT

(English)

You will have tremendous monetary success.

GRAY

(English) Graye, Grey

Wedded bliss and many children are in your future.

GRAYSON

(English) Graeson

You will be snubbed by a friend. Don't worry; you're better off without him.

GREGORY

(Greek) Greggory; Greg, Gregg

A surprising experience will cause you to dramatically change your current plans.

GRIFFIN

(Welsh) Griffen, Griffon; Griff

You will live an unconventional but truly satisfying life.

GUS

(Scandinavian)

Good fortune in business is fated for you.

GUTHRIE

(German, Irish) Guthry

You will be publicly honored for a heroic action.

GUY

(French) Guye

A dark-eyed stranger will cause you to unravel. This will be a difficult but enlightening experience.

GIRL NAMES

HADLEY

(English)

You will cultivate a lasting friendship with a very influential individual.

HAIDEE

(English)

Excessive spending will leave you dodging creditors.

HAILEY

(English) Hailee, Hailie, Haleigh, Haley, Halie, Halle, Hallie, Haylee, Hayley, Haylie

You will enjoy simple pleasures and lazy afternoons.

HANNAH

(Hebrew) Hanna

Good luck will favor you throughout your life.

HARMONY

(Latin)

A charming and attentive lover will quench your mental and physical desires.

HARPER

(English)

You will raise lovable but mischievous children.

HAYDEN

(English)

A slow but steady improvement will be made to your
current circumstances.

HAZEL

(English)

You will have a contented family life.

HEATHER

(Scottish)

Indiscretion will hamper your success.

HEIDI

(German)

Burgeoning popularity is in your future. Don't forget about
the people who got you there.

HELEN

(Greek) Helena

People will try to outshine you, but remember:
You are a star.

HILARY

(Latin) Hillary

You will battle a major setback and win.

HOLLY

(English)

A difficult situation will require a combination of strength and grace to resolve.

HONOR

(Latin)

You will make a fast friend who will bring out the very best in you.

HOPE

(Anglo-Saxon)

Success on an important project will come more easily than you expected.

BOY NAMES

HAINES

(German) Hanes, Haynes

You will spend many pleasant hours with your beloved.

HAMISH

(Scottish)

A new, interesting opportunity will wrench you from boredom.

HANS

(Scandinavian) Hants, Hanz

An unexpected encounter will lead to a profitable business relationship.

HARDEN

(English) Hardin, Hardyn

Your career will take a surprising turn, and you will make more money than you expected.

HARRISON

(English) Harrisson; Harris, Harriss, Harry

You will be blessed with good health and a lasting marriage.

HARRY

(English)

A new business enterprise will challenge you but ultimately reward you.

HAYDEN

(English) Haydan, Haydin

News from afar will change your perspective on a pressing matter.

HAYES

(English) Haiz, Hays

You will find yourself in an embarrassing situation. It's not as bad as you think.

HEATH

(English)

A risky undertaking will bring you great joy but little money.

HECTOR

(Greek)

A brief stint of ill luck is in store for you. Don't take any risks or make any major decisions for a while.

HENDRIK

(Dutch) Hendric, Hendrick

Your early success in business will bring you much leisure time later in life.

HENRY

(German) Hank, Harry

A life-altering adventure in a foreign land is in your future.

HEWITT

(German) Hewett

You will receive an unexpected legacy. Make good use of it, and you will never live in want.

HOGAN

(Irish) Hogen

A positive outcome will be the result of a complicated situation.

HOLDEN

(English) Holdin, Holdon

Your confidence in a proposed endeavor is unfounded. Do
your research before making any investments.

HOWELL

(Welsh) Howel

You will make an unfortunate social gaffe that will be the
subject of neighborhood gossip. Go about business as
usual, and it will soon be forgotten.

HUGH

(English) Hew

An unexpected gift from an estranged friend will warm
your cold heart.

HUNTER

(English)

You will never be without the love of a woman.

HUTTON

(English)

Follow your instincts, and luxury will be yours to enjoy.

HYDE

(English)

An unexpected companion will bring you great joy
and laughter.

GIRL NAMES

IDA

(German)

You will soon be rid of the negative forces around you.

ILANA

(Hebrew)

Your time and money will be wisely spent.

ILSA

(German) Ilse

Temptation will lure you into an unsavory situation.
Think before you act.

IMANI

(Arabic)

A foolhardy romance will get you into hot water.

INDIA

(Sanskrit)

Your pockets will be weighted down with wealth.

INEZ

(Spanish) Ines

Envy will tarnish a friendship. Try not to covet.

INGRID

(Norse)

A sudden call to action will ignite a fading passion.

IRENE

(Greek)

The solution to a lifelong mystery will bring you peace of mind.

IRIS

(Greek)

You carry a burden too heavy for you to bear alone. Ask others for help, or you will suffer.

ISABEL

(Spanish) Isabelle; Izzie, Izzy

The outcome of an important issue will surprise and please you.

ISABELLA

(Italian) Izabella

Major career success and public acclaim are fated for you.

ISADORA

(Latin)

Worry and anxiety over a current endeavor are unfounded. Success stands at your doorstep.

ISIS

(Egyptian)
A sudden resolution will end a long-endured problem.

IVANA

(Slavic)
You will be publicly recognized for your work in
the community.

IVY

(English)
A particularly exciting life is forecast for you.

BOY NAMES

IAN

(Scottish) Ean
You will make a name for yourself professionally and will
be well respected by your colleagues.

IBSEN

(Danish) Ibsan, Ibsin, Ibson
Your flexibility will make a sticky situation much more
bearable for all parties involved. It will not go unnoticed.

IDAN

(Hebrew)

Anticipate a showdown with your supervisor. Stick to your guns, and your demands will be met.

IGNACIO

(Spanish)

Unyielding passion is your blessing and your curse. In a risky investment, it will be your downfall; in a personal affair, your salvation.

IMRE

(Hungarian)

You will be rewarded for your work in your community.

INGMAR

(Norse) Ingemar

You are fated to father many children.

INGRAM

(German) Ingraham, Ingrim

A period of unfortunate events will lead to an advantageous opportunity.

INNES

(Scottish)

Some may call you stingy, but your prudent handling of your financial affairs will enable you to have a very comfortable retirement.

IRA

(Hebrew)

Physical danger of some sort lurks in your near future.
Watch your step!

IRVING

(English)

When you most need it, money, as if by magic, will come
your way.

IRWIN

(English) Erwin, Erwyn, Irwyn

An issue will cause you tremendous worry. Take a
step back. In the grand scheme of things, it's of
little consequence.

ISAAC

(Hebrew) Issac; Ike, Zack; Isaak (German), Isak (Russian), Izak (Polish), Ysaac (Spanish)

You will enjoy the company of your friends and will
laugh often.

ISAIAH

(Hebrew) Izaiah; Isai; Isaia (Italian), Ysais (Spanish)

A walk on the beach will unexpectedly inspire you.
Follow the muse, and you will meet with
unanticipated success.

ISANDRO

(Spanish)

Only when you free yourself from the golden handcuffs
will you find true happiness.

ISIDORE

(Greek) Dore, Dory, Izzy; Isidoro (Italian), Ysidor (Spanish)

An older woman will teach you an important lesson.
Pass it on.

IVAN

(Russian) Van

A childhood ambition will finally be realized
in adulthood.

GIRL NAMES

JACQUELINE

(French) Jacquelyn, Jaqueline; Jackie, Jacqui

Through diligence and painstaking care, you are in store for a significant financial gain.

JADE

(Spanish) Jada, Jaida

Beware. Jealous associates my try to sabotage a current project.

JADEN

(Hebrew) Jadyn, Jaiden, Jaidyn, Jayden

The gods have heard your prayers. The universe is conspiring to bring you good things.

JAMIE

(Hebrew) Jaime, Jaimee

You will receive news that will have a significant advantageous effect on your circumstances.

JANE

(Hebrew) Jayne; Janie

To finally move forward in your life, you will need to make amends for a past wrong.

JASMINE

(Persian) Jazmin, Jazmine, Jazmyn

An important career achievement will bring you respect and satisfaction.

JENNA

(English)

Once you break free from restrictive family ties, you will reach a long-sought-after goal.

JENNIFER

(Welsh) Jenifer, Genifer, Gennifer; Jen, Jenn, Jenny

You are due for a change of scenery. Don't fight it. The result will be a pleasant one.

JESSICA

(Hebrew) Jess, Jessie

You are overworked and underpaid. But rest assured, career salvation is on the way.

JOANNA

(English) Joana

A brief period of chaos and uncertainty will be followed by a long period of peace.

JOCELYN

(Latin) Joselyn, Joslyn

You are destined to be lucky in love.

JODY

(Hebrew) Jodie, Jodi

An opportunity for a significant life change will present itself. Wait and evaluate before you make any final decisions. Circumstances may shift.

JORDAN

(Hebrew) Jordyn

Beware of excessive flattery. Someone is up to something.

JOSEPHINE

(French) Jo, Jojo, Josie

You will have a disagreeable experience with a close friend. Don't let it turn your heart cold.

JOY

(Latin)

An educated risk will garner rich returns.

JUDITH

(Hebrew) Judy

Your financial woes will eventually come to an end. Prosperity is in your future.

JULES

(Latin)

You will find great happiness in love.

JULIA

(Latin)

An important project will temporarily derail before it gets on track. Stick with it. The outcome will be a good one.

JULIANA

(Latin) Julianna, Julianne

A good friend will help lighten the burden you are currently shouldering alone.

JULIE

(English)

You will be blessed with a happy home and many loving, obedient children.

JULIET

(French) Juliette

You are a woman of great social distinction.

BOY NAMES

JACKSON

(English) Jack

Impulsivity and hasty decisions can be dangerous. Success will come to you only after you spend some time truly considering your options.

JACOB

(Hebrew) Jakob, Jakobe; Jake

Your intellectual thinking and good judgment will take you to the top and keep you there.

JAMES

(Hebrew) Jamie

Your reliability will keep people coming back to you—professionally and personally.

JARED

(Hebrew)

You've allowed others to carry a burden that should have been borne by you. It's time to shoulder the load yourself.

JASON

(Greek)

You will marry young and will weather initial difficulties due to your age and inexperience. Time will bring confidence, security, and happiness.

JAVIER

(Spanish)

A steadfast friend will get you out of some serious trouble. Take advantage of your second chance. They don't come often.

JAYDEN

(Hebrew) Jaden, Jadon, Jadyn, Jaeden, Jaydon

Step up and lead your own army, or you forever will be taking orders instead of giving them.

JEFFREY

(English) Geoffrey; Geoff, Jeff

Someone will overshadow you at work. Step out into the light, and people will take notice of you and your abilities.

JEREMIAH

(Hebrew)

Your keen perception and awareness give you incredible social intelligence. This will serve you well in an awkward and precarious entanglement.

JEREMY

(English)

Your vivid imagination will create difficulties in a romantic relationship. Don't conjure up problems where there are none.

JESSE

(Hebrew) Jessie

A heated encounter at work will escalate unless you give credit where credit is due.

JESUS

(Hebrew)

Your perseverance and dedication will get you through a difficult period.

JOEL

(Hebrew)

Sharing confidences will sully a friendship. Make amends, and the damage will be minimal.

JONATHAN

(Hebrew) Johnathon, Jonathon; John, Johnny, Johnnie, Jon, Jonnie, Jonny

Your opinions are appreciated if presented with tact. Remember this when discussing a team project, or success will be hard won.

JORDAN

(Hebrew) Jordyn

You are capable of tremendous success. But you'll never taste it unless you start believing in yourself and your abilities.

JOSE

(Spanish)

Women love you. But remember, use good judgment.

JOSEPH

(Hebrew) Yosef; Joe, Joey

You will be blessed with a loving wife and
happy marriage.

JOSHUA

(Hebrew) Josh

Embrace an unexpected opportunity, and you will finally
taste success.

JUAN

(Spanish)

Surprising news will bring you great joy.

JULIAN

(Greek)

Before you commit yourself to an endeavor, do some
research. Someone's not telling you everything.

JUSTIN

(Latin)

The completion of your business dealings will leave you
a rich man.

GIRL NAMES

KAREN

(Greek) Caryn, Caren

You will reunite with an old friend who will quickly become a new lover.

KATRINA

(German)

You will have an unorthodox but very happy and contented marriage.

KAYLA

(Arabic, Hebrew)

Shush! Idle gossip will get you into big trouble with a friend.

KAYLEE

(American) Kailee, Kailey, Kaleigh, Kaley, Kali, Kallie

Indecision may cost you a rare opportunity. Trust your gut.

KEIRA

(Irish)

Watch your step! You will go through a brief period where you will be susceptible to minor accidents. Anticipate skinned knees.

KELLY

(Irish) Kellie

A new investment will bring you monetary security.

KELSEY

(Scottish)

You will receive an invitation to an exclusive event that will increase your social status.

KENDALL

(English) Kendal

A cross-country journey will reveal the opportunity of a lifetime.

KENDRA

(English)

You are struggling with your current career choice. An influential and experienced person will help you find the right answer.

KENNEDY

(Irish) Kennedi

You are destined for dramatic or artistic work.

KIARA

(Irish)

A pet project will evolve into more than you expected.

KILEY

(Irish) Kylie, Kylee, Kyleigh, Kylie

You will find happiness and satisfaction in home life.

KIMBERLY

(English) Kim, Kym

An unexpected legacy from a distant relative will ease your financial woes.

KIRSTEN

(Greek, Scandinavian) Kiersten

A drastic improvement in your living conditions is predicted.

KRISTA

(Czech) Christa

Time spent on a problematic venture will not be time wasted.

KRISTEN

(Greek) Kristin; Kris

Good health and a satisfying love life are destined for you.

KYA

(African)

An important decision will meet with opposition from friends and family. Stick to your guns. You know what's best for you.

KYLA

(Irish)

A solution to your current problem can be found at home.

KYRA

(Greek)

An unexpected opportunity will shift your priorities.

BOY NAMES

KAI

(Welsh)

Slow down. Take a breath. Or your intensity and
extremism will inhibit you from true success.

KANE

(Welsh) Cain, Kayne

The success and ease of a new project will reflect
well on you.

KARL

(German)

Your career path, though circuitous and bumpy, will lead
you in the right direction. Stay the course, and you won't
regret it.

KEATON

(English)

A selfish streak will cause problems in your private affairs.
Change your attitude, or suffer a solitary future.

KEEGAN

(Irish)

You were wronged. It's true. But don't burn the bridge. You will
need it in the future.

KEIFER

(German) Keiffer

Your confidence is a blessing and a curse. It both attracts and
intimidates people. Learn how to bridge that gap, and you'll
have even greater success.

KEITH

(Welsh)

You have a tendency toward cynicism and negativity.
Be sure to see the silver lining.

KELLEN

(Irish)

You will reconcile with an estranged family member.

KENDRICK

(Irish)

You will eventually hold an influential position at work.

KENNETH

(Irish) Ken, Kennie

A frustrating delay will bring an unexpected opportunity.

KENT

(Welsh)

Your inner self is in conflict with your outer self. Balance the two, and you will find happiness.

KEVIN

(Irish)

Nobody's perfect. Accept your mistakes and inadequacies, or you will never be truly content.

KIPP

(English) Kip

Your intensity, if properly focused, will bring you prosperity and good health.

KURT

(Latin)

Stay the course, and your greatest ambition will be realized.

KYLE

(Irish)

You will be saddled with many new responsibilities but will be handsomely compensated for them.

GIRL NAMES

LACEY

(Latin) Laci, Lacie

Your enthusiasm and vigor will lead you to prosperity.

LANA

(Latin)

Unforeseen difficulties will delay a project. Remain flexible, and they won't hamper your success.

LANE

(English) Lanie, Laney

Your secret plans will be realized.

LARISSA

(Greek)

A questionable business associate will prove to be unreliable. You're better off without him.

LAURA

(Latin)

A most unusual but auspicious opportunity will present itself to you. Take it!

LAUREL

(Latin)

Hasty decisions will impede your success. Be more
deliberate in your actions, and you can turn it around.

LAUREN

(English) Lauryn, Loren

Anticipate a sudden but advantageous change
of environment.

LAYLA

(Hebrew) Laila

Unusual new friends will help you rediscover a part of
yourself you thought forever lost.

LEAH

(Hebrew) Lea

A long-lost lover will surface after many years. He's here
to stay.

LESLIE

(Scottish) Lesley, Lesly

Your financial worries will be short-lived.

LILLIAN

(Latin)

Reexamine your current plan of attack. There's
something you're missing.

LILY

(Latin) Lillie, Lilly

An important negotiation will prove successful if you don't wilt under the pressure. Stay strong, and you'll get a fair deal.

LINDA

(Spanish) Lynda

Your business affairs will be a disappointment, but you'll have great luck in affairs of the heart.

LINDSEY

(English) Lindsay, Lyndsey, Linsey

An unexpected hardship will be made tolerable by the support of a new friend.

LOLA

(Spanish)

You will recover something of great value that you thought forever lost.

LOUISE

(German)

Tremendous satisfaction will be taken from your efforts made in the community.

LUCY

(Latin) Lucie

A current problem will have an unusual but entirely palatable resolution.

LUZ

(Spanish)

You will take great pleasure in the company of children.

LYDIA

(Greek) Lidia

Keep your eyes peeled. Favorable news will arrive by mail.

BOY NAMES

LAMAR

(Latin)

Your good fortune will come in the form of steadfast friends.

LANCE

(German)

You need not worry about the future. The rough road you are navigating will eventually smooth out.

LANDON

(English) Landen, Landyn

Your creative prowess will bring you much career success.

LANGSTON

(English)

You will use your intelligence and wit to good advantage.

LAWRENCE

(Latin) Laurence; Larry

Working for a tyrannical boss is a choice. Choose another option, and you will be freed of stress and anxiety.

LEE

(English) Leigh

Your charm and magnetism will get you into trouble. Be careful.

LELAND

(English)

Hasty decisions lead to disappointing results. Think things through more carefully, or you will continue to be dissatisfied.

LEON

(Greek)

An unanticipated detour will take you on the adventure of your life.

LEONARDO

(Italian)

The solution to a pressing problem will reveal itself to you through a child.

LEVI

(Hebrew)

Living the high life will drain your energy and your wallet. Slow down before you run into any real problems.

LEWIS

(German) Louis; Lew, Lou

A lifelong dream will be realized only if you truly give yourself a chance. Stop distracting yourself and do it already.

LIAM

(Irish)

Pleasant diversions and simple pleasures will keep you happy.

LLOYD

(English)

Your thirst for knowledge will only be satiated if you return to school. Stop telling yourself it's not possible. It is.

LOGAN

(Irish)

You will have a healthy and happy married life.

LORENZO

(Spanish)

You are due for a period of hard work, but it will not go unrewarded.

LUCA

(Italian)

A most fortunate business deal is in your future.

LUCAS

(Greek) Lukas

Luck in love is augured for you.

LUIS

(Spanish)

A drastic change of plans is necessary to achieve
your goal.

LUKE

(Latin)

Your stress and anxiety will be eased once you right a
past wrong.

GIRL NAMES

MACKENZIE

(Irish) Makenzie, McKenzie

Relax. You will have control over an important family decision.

MADELINE

(Greek) Madelyn, Madelynn, Madilyn, Madeleine

A difficult endeavor will earn you more respect than money.

MADISON

(English) Madisen, Madisyn, Madyson

Inconsequential annoyances will surface at the worst possible time. Don't give them more energy than they deserve.

MAKAYLA

(American) Micaela, Michaela, Mikaela, Mikayla

No matter how great the pull, resist an unexpected temptation, or a relationship will suffer.

MARGARET

(Greek) Margot, Margo, Peggy

Breathe easy. The chaos that is your personal affairs will soon subside.

MARIA

(Hebrew)

A change of career will be the best decision you ever made.

MARIAH

(Hebrew)

Anticipate a loving mate and a happy marriage.

MARISSA

(Latin) Marisa

You will question advice from a friend regarding an important matter. Don't. She's right.

MARY

(Hebrew)

Buckle up! A whirlwind year will be just the beginning of your career success.

MAYA

(Greek)

Your uncertain living situation will be resolved after the new year.

MEGAN

(Greek) Meagan, Meghan

The end of your personal tribulations will coincide with the long-overdue end of a romantic relationship.

MELANIE

(Greek) Melany; Mel

You will accomplish something you once thought impossible.

MELISSA

(Greek)

A quarrel with a lover will lead to a new discovery.

MEREDITH

(Welsh)

Congratulations. An enterprising business deal will be a profitable one.

MIA

(Italian) Miah

You will have faithful friends and adoring lovers.

MICHELLE

(French)

Questionable business practices will get you into trouble. Steer clear of bad influences.

MIRANDA

(Latin)

The sad end of one affair will open the door to another.

MOLLY

(Irish) Mollie

Decisions made in anger will come back to haunt you.

MONICA

(Greek)

You will stand on morally questionable ground. Listen to your conscience. It will guide you in the right direction.

MORGAN

(Welsh)

A career failure will unexpectedly pave the way for a success.

BOY NAMES

MALCOLM

(Scottish)

In your quest for love, you must overcome a bitter rival.

MANUEL

(Hebrew) Manny

A convoluted situation will sort itself out in time.

MARCEL

(French)

Someone of consequence will walk into your life masquerading as a vagabond. Don't judge on appearances, or you will miss out on a rare opportunity.

MARCUS

(Latin) Markus; Marc, Mark

Family squabbles will frequently color your mood. Shake it off.

MARIO

(Italian)

Look out for the wiles of a woman with dark eyes. Her intentions are not true.

MARSHALL

(French)

A great honor will be bestowed upon you.

MARTIN

(Latin)

You're a smart cookie. The more you play dumb, the more people are going to believe it.

MASON

(French)

Stop hiding. A public humiliation will be forgotten.

MATTHEW

(Hebrew) Mathew; Matt, Mattie

A yearlong sabbatical will teach you more than decades of schooling.

MAURICE

(Latin)

You will marry a young lady of ample means.

MAXWELL

(English)

A political ambition soon will be realized.

MICAH

(Hebrew)

Your athletic prowess will bring you great prosperity.

MICHAEL

(Hebrew) Mike

A change of environment will bring you tremendous happiness.

MIGUEL

(Spanish)

If you're not careful, something you've worked diligently to gain will be lost.

MILES

(German) Myles

You're a gypsy, but true love will bring you home.

MILO

(German)

People underestimate your intellect. Prove them wrong.

MILTON

(English)

Monotony will be the death of you. Take that trip, and you won't regret it.

MITCHELL

(English) Mitch

Your determined nature will bring you tremendous financial success.

MURPHY

(Irish)

Your marriage will be a long and lasting one.

GIRL NAMES

NADIA

(Slavic)

A long journey will be draining but fruitful.

NADINE

(French)

You will have a successful career in the performing arts, particularly dancing.

NANCY

(English)

Your generosity will earn you a place in the hearts of many.

NAOMI

(Hebrew) Noemi, Nyomi

Your beauty will open a door for you, but it's your intelligence that will get you through it.

NATALIE

(Latin) Natalee, Nataly; Natalia (Russian)

The winter season will prove to be a particularly productive time for you. Anticipate good news on Christmas.

NATASHA

(Russian) Tasha

An unexpected gift from an old friend will bring you
great joy.

NELLIE

(English)

Your lighthearted nature will delight many suitors.

NEVAEH

(American)

You are a divine inspiration to family, friends,
and associates.

NEVE

(Hebrew)

A well-planned endeavor will have a promising outcome.

NICOLE

(French) Nichole, Nicolelle

You will win a seemingly arbitrary bet that will change
your future.

NINA

(Spanish, Hebrew)

Your confidence and daring will bring you much
financial success.

NOELLE

(French)

Your energetic nature and enthusiasm will reinvigorate a dying project.

NORA

(Greek) Norah

You will be a loving mother to many doting children.

BOY NAMES

NASH

(English)

A casual conversation will spark an idea. Follow it through, and you'll meet with great success.

NASIR

(Arabic)

Language will play a key role in your career.

NATHAN

(Hebrew) Nathen

A journey will be rough at the start. But don't turn back. There's something waiting for you at the end.

NATHANIEL

(Hebrew) Nathanael, Nathanial; Nate

Your originality is your ticket to success. New ideas and innovative approaches to problems will bring you prosperity and respect.

NELSON

(English)

A goal will be realized only if you put your best effort forward.

NEVILLE

(French)

You will find true happiness by the sea.

NICHOLAS

(Greek) Nicolas, Nikolas; Nic, Nico, Niko

You will be victorious over an adversary.

NIGEL

(English)

A stubborn streak will keep you from reaching your full potential.

NOAH

(Hebrew)

The resolution to a lifelong problem will bring you great peace.

NOE

(Spanish)

Riches and pleasures are augured for you.

NOEL

(French)

You will be rewarded for work well done.

NOLAN

(Irish)

When faced with an important decision, look only to yourself for the answer.

NORMAN

(English)

Regrets haunt you. Let them go, or you'll never find peace.

NORRIS

(English)

You are destined for a happy home life.

GIRL NAMES

OCEANA

(Greek)

A love of nature will unite you with your mate. Mad love will be made in the shadow of a tree.

OCTAVIA

(Latin)

On the eighth day of the eighth month, an unusual opportunity will reveal itself to you.

ODELE

(Greek)

Tune in. Music will be tremendously influential in your life.

ODESSA

(Greek)

You will go on a great quest that will reveal the answer to a long-asked question.

ODETTE

(German)

The good girl in you wants to be practical; the bad girl wants to take risks. Find a balance, and you will also find success.

OLIVE

(Latin)

You're too subtle. No one will know what you want unless you tell them. Just say it clearly, succinctly. You'll be amazed by the results.

OLIVIA

(Latin)

A new business venture will flourish.

OLYMPIA

(Greek)

Your partner thinks you're a gift from the gods.

OPAL

(Hindi)

Your delicate handling of sticky situations and difficult people will earn you a raise at work.

OPHELIA

(Greek)

You will have great success in a career that celebrates your helpful, caring nature.

BOY NAMES

OCTAVIO

(Latin)

You will discover new abilities that will create a profitable opportunity for you.

ODIN

(Scandinavian)

Work out a misunderstanding before it escalates into something irreparable.

OGDEN

(English) Ogdon; Oggie

Intelligence and determination will bring you much career success.

OLIVER

(Latin) Ollie

Your loving nature will pave the way for romance.

OMAR

(Arabic) Omari

A return to your spiritual self will fill the void you're feeling.

OREN

(Hebrew)

Anticipate news that will significantly change your life.

ORION

(Greek)

A brief period of financial or social distress is foretold.

ORLANDO

(German)

A trusted friend will betray you. Be careful what you share and with whom.

OSBORN

(Scandinavian, English)

A new venture, be it personal or professional, will be successful.

OSCAR

(Scandinavian)

A problem that has caused you much worry will soon resolve itself.

OTIS

(Greek)

Travel with friends and family will serve as a nice distraction from a pressing worry.

OTTO

(German)

Hard times lie ahead. It would be wise to limit your spending.

OWEN

(Irish)

You will achieve a long-sought-after goal due to persistence and patience.

OZZIE

(English)

An unexpected trip brought about by surprising news will yield a profitable opportunity.

GIRL NAMES

PAIGE

(English) Page

True happiness will be found on the home front.

PALOMA

(Spanish)

A new romance is about to take flight. Fly, bird, fly.

PAMELA

(Greek) Pam

Hold tight. The emotional storms that have been dampening your mood are about the clear.

PARIS

(French)

You are destined for gratuitous wealth.

PARKER

(English)

You will succeed in a career that celebrates your creative abilities.

PASHA

(Greek)

You will never live in want of love or money.

PATRICE

(French)

You will do great things with your time, money, and abilities.

PATRICIA

(Latin) Pat, Patsy, Pattie, Patty, Patti

Your vigilance and dedication to a cause will be rewarded by subtle but distinct social change.

PAULA

(Latin) Polly; Paola (Italian), Paulette (French), Paulina (Slavic)

Though sometimes isolating, your self-reliance will bring you great professional success.

PAYTON

(Irish) Peyton

Your confidence and strong will challenge and intimidate, but ultimately inspire, those around you.

PEARL

(Latin)

Your loyalty and affection are prized by your friends. You will never be lonely or in want of companionship.

PENELOPE

(Greek)

Your cleverness and capability will bring you success in your professional endeavors.

PHOEBE

(Greek)

You're a star in whatever you do. Success should not feel
unusual to you.

PILAR

(Spanish)

You are the foundation that holds your family together.
And even though they don't say it enough, you are loved
and appreciated for it.

PIPER

(English)

You will not suffer needlessly. A difficult period will result
in a life-changing epiphany.

PORTIA

(Latin)

You will make a new and unusual friend who will change
your way of thinking.

PRISCILLA

(Latin)

Your experience will make you invaluable on an upcom-
ing project. Use it to your advantage.

BOY NAMES

PABLO

(Spanish)

Beware. Unless you speak up, a colleague will profit from your ideas and hard work.

PACO

(Italian)

You will find something that you thought forever lost.

PALMER

(English)

You need to be more aggressive in order to achieve your current goals.

PANCHO

(Spanish)

Use discretion when discussing personal matters, or a relationship will suffer.

PARKER

(English)

Good news. An impulsive risk will yield significant returns.

PARNELL

(French)

Your difficulties will be easily overcome.

PASCAL

(French)

Relief from financial stress will arrive just in time.

PATRICK

(Latin) Pat, Paddy

You will enter a period of ill luck. Be cautious when dealing with money matters.

PAUL

(Latin), Paulo (Spanish)

Don't succumb to heedless indulgences, or your bank account will suffer.

PAXTON

(Latin)

You will help estranged friends reconcile.

PAYTON

(English) Peyton

A new endeavor will be a great success.

PEDRO

(Spanish)

You will lose a lover through foolhardiness.

PERRY

(English)

An ill-conceived plan should be aborted. The result will not be as you'd hoped.

PETER

(Greek) Pete; Pierre (French)

You will have good fortune in financial matters but bad luck in affairs of the heart.

PHILIP

(Greek) Phillip; Phil

You will be the victim of a woman's whimsy.

PHOENIX

(Latin)

You are destined for a loving relationship and financial security.

PIERCE

(English)

Change your course of action, or die of boredom.

PORTER

(Latin)

You will receive a gift from a new acquaintance.

PRESCOTT

(English)

Your thoughtlessness will alienate a good friend. But it's not too late to make amends.

PRESTON

(English)

You will be complacent no more. Significant personal and professional changes are afoot.

PRICE

(Welsh)

You are due for a period of ill luck. Take precautions, and avoid making any significant decisions for a while.

GIRL NAMES

QUEEN

(English) Queenie

You were born a leader, and it shows in everything you do.

QUENBY

(Scandinavian) Quinby

Your love life will never be without fun and adventure.

QUINCY

(French)

The summer will be a productive time for you.
Take advantage of it.

QUINN

(Irish)

You are about to enter a particularly auspicious period.
Now is the time to take a risk or start a new endeavor.

QUINTANA

(Spanish)

Ill fortune lurks in the distance, but you'll be fine as long
as you take the proper precautions.

QUINTESSA

(Latin)

An all-encompassing project will leave you physically spent but financially and emotionally fulfilled.

BOY NAMES

QADIR

(Arabic)

A period of bad luck lurks in the future. Anticipate complications and annoyances.

QAMAR

(Arabic)

Beware. A trusted friend may not have your best interests at heart.

QUADE

(Latin)

Your character is in question. You need to set the record straight or suffer a setback.

QUAY

(French)

Questionable choices may get you into trouble. Consider your actions wisely.

QUENNEL

(French)

You need to address your anger issues, or problems will continue to mount.

QUENTIN

(Latin) Quinten, Quintin, Quinton; Quint

A unique opportunity will present itself. Take it!

QUILLAN

(Irish)

Anticipate an economic upswing in your financial affairs.

QUIMBY

(Norse)

Fluctuations in market conditions have already gotten the better of you. Invest wisely.

QUINCE

(Latin)

Stay focused on your goal despite the onslaught of distractions, and you will succeed.

QUINCY

(French)

Questionable conduct will get you into hot water at work. Pull it together.

QUINLAN

(Irish)

Difficulties in business and love will soon subside.

QUINN

(Irish)

You are embedded in a predicament that only you
can rectify.

GIRL NAMES

RACHEL

(Hebrew) Rachael; Raquel, Rachelle (French)

You are destined for marital bliss. Your wedding will be just the beginning of the love affair.

RAINA

(German) Reanna, Rayna

Your thrift will keep you out of financial trouble.

RAJA

(Arabic)

A current undertaking is off-track, but there's still time to reconfigure your strategy.

RAMONA

(Spanish)

Lace up your boots, a new adventure is on the horizon.

RANDY

(English) Randi

Unexpected guests will overstay their welcome.

RAVEN

(English)

You will be recognized for your work in the community.

REAGAN

(Irish)

Your current project will end successfully.

REBECCA

(Hebrew) Rebeca, Rebekah

Your ambition will exhaust you but will keep you from complacency.

REECE

(Welsh) Reese

You have been a heroic friend, but it's time to turn the attention to yourself.

REGINA

(Latin)

Family struggles will dissipate once you start communicating with each other.

REMI

(French)

The road to success can be long, so it's unwise to rush it. Slow down before you overheat.

RENEE

(French) Renae

You will reach a turning point in your life. With it comes a level of success that you never imagined.

RHONDA

(Welsh)

Don't worry; it won't be long until someone special takes an interest in you.

RILEY

(Irish) Reilly, Rylee, Ryleigh, Rylie

You are not an island. A difficult endeavor will only be successful if you ask for help.

RITA

(Sanskrit)

Unfortunately, your success depends equally on ability and politics. You've got the former under control but need to work a bit on how to handle the latter.

ROBIN

(English) Robyn

You will shed your old skin and search for something new. If nothing fits quite right, don't worry. It's not you; you're simply looking in the wrong places.

ROCHELLE

(French)

A friendship will become more of a crutch than a relationship. When that happens, it's time to start experiencing life on your own.

ROMY

(French)

Nothing goes smoothly. Until you accept this fact, you will never be truly happy.

RORY

(Irish)

You will find love once you have the courage to open your heart.

ROSE

(Latin), Rosa (Italian, Spanish)

The world weighs you down. Start letting things go, and you'll get that skip back in your step.

ROSELYN

(Spanish)

Do not fear change in your life. With it will come happy times and good fortune.

ROSEMARY

(English)

A journey to your childhood home will show you just how far you've come.

ROXANA

(Persian) Roxanna, Roxanne

You can start loosening your belt. Your financial woes are coming to an end.

RUBY

(French) Rubi

Stop worrying. You have triumphed over misfortune in the past. It will happen again.

RUTH

(Hebrew) Ruthie

Your effort on a project will go unrewarded, but it will not go unnoticed.

RYAN

(Irish) Ryann

You are due for some unexpected success.

BOY NAMES

RAFAEL

(Spanish), Raphael (Hebrew)

With patience and focus, you will achieve your goal despite setbacks and complications.

RAFFERTY

(Irish)

After years of silence, you will reconcile with an estranged friend.

RALPH

(English), Raoul (French)

A new approach will get a significantly delayed project back on track.

RAMSEY

(English) Ramsay

A period of ill fortune looms. Change and risks are not advised. Don't make any major decisions or investments until your luck has clearly changed.

RANDALL

(English)

Living a life of extravagance will affect your health. Be careful, or the damage will be permanent.

RAYMOND

(German) Ray; Ramon (Spanish)

You will be blessed with good health and prosperity.

REAGAN

(Irish)

You carry a dangerous secret that should not be shared, no matter how great the temptation.

REECE

(Welsh) Reese, Rhys

A team project will bring great financial reward and honor.

REED

(English) Reid

You are fated for happiness on the home front.

REMY

(French)

Wise up! You will miss a significant opportunity due to foolhardiness.

RENE

(French)

Your romantic affairs are complicated by apprehension. Stop worrying. She likes you.

REX

(Latin)

Be careful. Your natural impulsiveness could lead to financial distress.

REYNARD

(German)

You will have great success in a questionable endeavor.

RHETT

(Welsh)

Stop wasting your time and energy on inconsequential and trivial pursuits. Greater matters need your attention.

RICHARD

(English), Ricardo (Spanish)

You will have several significant financial setbacks.
Be smarter with your money, and you'll get through it.

RIDLEY

(English)

Exciting news is on the way.

RILEY

(Irish) Reilly, Rylee

Negative forces are mounting against you.
Watch your back.

ROBERT

(English), Roberto (Italian, Spanish), Rupert (German)

You will have to endure a period of heated quarrels
before the road to romance smoothes out.

ROCCO

(German, Italian)

An advantageous new friendship will change the course
of your career.

RODNEY

(English)

You should select your companions more carefully or face
a sullied reputation.

RODRIGO

(Spanish)

Anticipate an embarrassing but inconsequential entanglement in an unpleasant circumstance.

ROGER

(German)

You will receive a long-desired gift from a family member.

ROLAND

(German), Rolando (Spanish)

Impulsive changes in your career will be detrimental.

ROMAN

(Latin)

You will be recognized for your efforts in the community.

RONALD

(Norse) Ron, Ronnie; Renaldo (Spanish)

Outside opinion will lead you astray on an important matter. Follow your instincts.

ROSS

(Scottish, Latin)

Be careful. Hubris will detract from work well done.

ROWAN

(English) Rohan

You are hiding something. This is doing you a disservice.
Take action, or live in want.

ROY

(French)

You will come out of a difficult situation with no damage
to your reputation.

RUBEN

(Hebrew)

You and your mate are well-suited. Anticipate a
lifelong romance.

RUSSELL

(French) Russ, Rusty

You are due for a period of great luck and prosperity.
Every area of your life will see improvement.

RYAN

(Irish)

Anticipate disputes with your lover. Having a gift on hand
probably isn't a bad idea.

RYDER

(English) Rider

Opportunity and good fortune are destined for you.

GIRL NAMES

SABINE

(Latin)

You will wear many career hats before you find the right fit.

SABRINA

(Latin)

Reach out. Your loving and supportive family wants to help you through the rough patches.

SADIE

(Hebrew)

You are destined for great love.

SALLY

(English) Sallie

You're an original and will be rewarded for your fresh ideas and creative approaches to problems.

SALMA

(Arabic)

You will profit from your sense of style and good taste.

SAMANTHA

(Aramaic) Sammie, Sammy

Unexpected fame will shock and delight you.

SANDRA

(Greek) Sandy

Your financial stress will be short-lived.

SARAH

(Hebrew) Sara

Your confidence combined with your abilities will make you shine at work.

SASHA

(Russian)

Unexpected business prospects are ripe for success.

SAVANNAH

(Spanish) Savana, Savanah, Savanna

You will have tremendous career fulfillment.

SCARLETT

(English) Scarlet

People will come to you specifically for your honesty. Don't start sugarcoating when a tough truth is what they need to hear.

SELENA

(Greek) Selina

Your calm presence and inherent peacefulness will help defuse a tense work environment.

SERENA

(Latin)

Your ability to find the comedy in life does more than simply entertain.

SHANNON

(Irish)

You are admired for the rare combination of keen intelligence and approachability.

SHARI

(French)

An insatiable hunger for adventure will take you to the most remote reaches of the globe.

SHARON

(Hebrew)

People should learn from you. Your open heart and ability to reach out to others sets you apart from the masses.

SHAUNA

(Hebrew) Shana

You are giving of your time and money. For this, you will be admired and respected.

SHELBY

(English)

You are fated for a home buzzing with children's laughter.

SIENNA

(Italian) Siena

You are a great beauty, but people admire and appreciate
you more for your humility.

SIERRA

(Irish)

A happy union and loving home are in your future.

SIMONE

(Hebrew)

Your quiet wisdom will keep you out of trouble.

SKYLER

(Dutch) Skylar

Loosen your grip. Your tendency to shelter and over-
protect isn't good for anyone involved.

SOFIA

(Greek) Sophia; Sophie

You will never be without love and affection.

STACEY

(Greek) Stacy

You are no longer fulfilled by the trappings of success.
Anticipate a return to your more spiritual self.

STELLA

(Latin)

A risky business venture will pay off.

STEPHANIE

(Greek) Stephany; Steph

You will mother many happy children.

SUMMER

(English)

A fresh look at an old problem will reveal the solution.

SUSAN

(Hebrew) Sue, Susie, Suzie

Your courage, love, and support will get you through a difficult time at home.

SYDNEY

(French) Sidney, Sydni, Sydnie; Sid, Syd

Your enthusiasm for a project will save it from the chopping block.

SYLVIA

(Latin) Silvia

You will learn a secret about a friend; use the utmost discretion to avoid embarrassment.

BOY NAMES

SALINGER

(French)

Ill-fortune lurks in the near future. Be cautious with your resources, and avoid taking any big risks or making any investments.

SALVADOR

(Spanish), Salvator (Latin), Salvatore (Italian)

You are destined for wealth and prestige.

SAMIR

(Arabic)

Your ambitions will soon be realized.

SAMSON

(Hebrew)

Positive change is afoot. Anticipate significant improvements in your circumstances or surroundings.

SAMUEL

(Hebrew) Sam, Sammy

Cheer up. More interesting and adventurous work is on the horizon.

SANFORD

(English)

You are due for a period of good fortune in both personal and professional matters.

SANTIAGO

(Spanish)

You will receive public acknowledgment for work well done.

SANTINO

(Spanish)

You are fated for domestic harmony and good health.

SANTOS

(Spanish)

Things aren't as bad as they seem. Tough times in your romantic relationship will be short-lived.

SASHA

(Russian)

New acquaintances will infuse some much-needed energy into your social circle.

SAUL

(Hebrew)

You will make significant progress on a project that has recently been delayed.

SAWYER

(English)

You are fated for a happy marriage.

SCOTT

(English)

Your circumstances may appear dim now, but your fortunes are indeed brightening.

SEAN

(Irish) Shaun, Shawn

Your occupation is ill-suited to you. A better match awaits.

SEBASTIAN

(Latin) Sabastian

Stay the course. You're on the right track; success is at hand.

SERGIO

(Italian, Spanish)

You will embark on an endeavor that is beyond your capabilities. Set realistic goals, or face disappointment.

SETH

(Hebrew)

Your career ambition will entail more effort to realize than you expected.

SHANE

(Irish) Shayne

An indiscretion will cause you only momentary embarrassment.

SHELDON

(English)

Your deepest desires will be realized sooner than you expect.

SIDNEY

(French) Sydney

A spell of difficult work will have positive results.

SIMON

(Hebrew)

A most fortunate change of circumstance is on the way.

SOLOMON

(Hebrew)

A period of good luck in money matters will help wipe out a growing debt.

SPENCER

(French) Spence

Pack your bags. An exotic locale and an exotic stranger await.

STANLEY

(English) Stan

Wait until after the new year to embark on a new career.

STEPHEN

(Greek) Stephan, Steven; Steve

Inconsequential worries distract you from what's really important. Focus on things you can control.

STERLING

(English)

Don't fret. Troubled waters in romance will eventually calm.

STUART

(Scottish)

Prepare for a radical change of circumstance.

SULLIVAN

(Irish) Sullie

Your financial worries are for naught. Money is in your future.

SVEN

(Scandinavian)

Think before you act. Foolhardy behavior will get you into hot water personally and professionally.

GIRL NAMES

TABITHA

(Aramaic)

A mad love will shake up your world.

TALIA

(Hebrew) Taliyah

Your devotion to friends and family is admirable, but don't forget about your own happiness.

TALLULAH

(Native American)

When financial success is no longer enough, you will turn your attention to more spiritual matters.

TAMARA

(Hebrew) Tammy

Stop questioning. A significant change of surroundings is for the best.

TANYA

(Russian) Tania

A creative business venture will bring you much success.

TARA

(Irish) Tera

You will lead your team to victory.

TATIANA

(Russian) Tatianna

You will parlay your ability to effectively articulate a
vision into a profitable career in communications.

TATUM

(English)

Your enthusiasm and passion for life inspire those
around you.

TAYLOR

(English) Tayler

You are fated for wedded bliss.

TERRELL

(Greek) Tyrell, Tyrelle

Your thick skin and hardy constitution make you a
perfect candidate for politics.

THEA

(Greek) Tea

Your reliability will earn you a steady stream of work and
many friends.

THERESA

(Greek) Teresa; Terry, Tess, Tessa

You will be blessed with good health and a sound mind.

TIFFANY

(Greek)

Lasting love is fated for you.

TONI

(Greek)

Though it will get off to a slow start, your career will flourish.

TORI

(English) Tory

You will amass great wealth.

TRACY

(Latin) Tracey, Traci

Your friends will be loyal and your husband faithful.

TRINITY

(Latin)

A hasty choice will turn out better than you expected.

TRISTA

(Latin)

You will go through quite an education. It won't seem like it at the time, but you will learn something that will come in handy later.

TYLER

(English)

A new relationship will open your mind and warm
your heart.

TYRA

(Scandinavian)

You're assertive and confident, two qualities that secure
your position as a leader.

BOY NAMES

TAJ

(Sanskrit)

Creature comforts and contentment are in your future.

TAMIR

(Hebrew)

A powerful person will give you an unexpected
opportunity.

TANNER

(English)

A beautiful and intelligent woman will forever steal your
heart and mind.

TATE

(English)

The time is nigh to seize advantageous business opportunities.

TAYLOR

(English)

A difficult period is finally coming to a close. Good times with friends and family are ahead.

TERRANCE

(Latin) Terrence; Terry

Peace and contentment will soon replace your anxiety and worry.

THADDEUS

(Aramaic) Tad, Thad

A unique and unexpected experience will open your eyes to a new opportunity.

THANE

(Scottish)

You will overcome current obstacles despite setbacks.

THEODORE

(Greek) Theo

Misfortune is fated for you unless every decision is made with extreme care.

THOMAS

(Aramaic, Greek) Tomas; Tom, Tommy

Marital happiness and spiritual fulfillment are fated for you.

THORNTON

(English)

Stop interfering in the affairs of others, or relationships will suffer.

TIMOTHY

(Greek) Tim, Timmy

Do not overextend yourself, or your current goals will not be met.

TOBIAS

(Hebrew) Toby

You will be most fortunate in matters of the heart.

TODD

(English) Tod

Unexpected news will necessitate foreign travel.

TRAVIS

(French)

A professional endeavor will reap great personal and financial rewards.

TRENTON

(English) Trent

Your excessive thrift may lose you a lover. There's a time and place for penny-pinching.

TREVOR

(Welsh) Trever

Leave bad habits behind, or your health will suffer.

TREY

(English)

An intriguing romantic encounter will zap your boredom.

TRISTAN

(Celtic) Tristen, Tristian, Tristin, Triston

A night out with old friends will be a welcome reprieve from loneliness.

TROY

(Irish)

A slew of unfortunate events will pepper an otherwise happy time. Focusing on the good will get you through the bad.

TUCKER

(English)

Exotic travels will open your eyes to a new way of thinking.

TURNER

(English)

You will successfully navigate mounting work obstacles.

TYLER

(English) Tylor; Ty

A dying soul will necessitate the rebirth of your
spiritual self.

TYSON

(English)

An unexpected change will turn a bad situation into a
tolerable one.

GIRL NAMES

ULA

(Irish)

Your struggle with a difficult problem will come to a successful end.

UMA

(Hindi)

Someone adores you but is afraid to admit it.

UMEKO

(Japanese)

Your determination will get you through the tail end of a draining project.

UNA

(Latin)

A new romance will provide you a much-needed distraction.

UNIQUE

(Latin)

Your worries are unnecessary. Life is good. Enjoy it.

UNITY

(English)

You will find happiness and satisfaction in motherhood.

URBANA

(Latin)

Good fortune in business is augured for you.

URI

(Hebrew)

Impulsive actions will get you into the kind of trouble you could do without. Think.

URSULA

(Greek) Ursa

An unexpected reunion will resolve a lingering family issue.

UTA

(German)

Your thirst for adventure will never be satiated—no matter what your age. For a successful marriage, your partner should share your passion.

BOY NAMES

UDALL

(English)

Difficult circumstances will demand your attention before they can be resolved.

ULRICH

(German)

Incisive action is the only way to avoid a mounting problem.

ULTMAN

(Hindi)

Professional changes are afoot. Don't run from new responsibilities. You can handle them.

ULYSSES

(Latin) Ulises

A financially advantageous opportunity will make you rich.

UMAR

(Hindi)

Reevaluate your relationships. Someone is untrue.

UMBERTO

(Italian)

When you stop asking, a nagging question will finally be answered.

UPTON

(English)

You will experience an extended spell of comfort and satisfaction. Enjoy it.

URIEL

(Hebrew) Uri

You are overextending yourself to the point of detriment. Learn to prioritize, or suffer big losses.

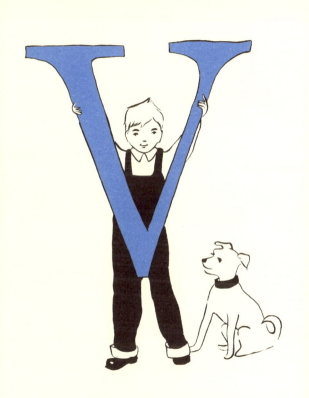

GIRL NAMES

VAIL

(English) Vale

A risky venture will prove to be even more of a success than you anticipated.

VALENTINA

(Latin)

Someone you meet socially will turn out to be of great help professionally.

VALERIE

(French) Val

An associate aims to do you harm. Beware of false fronts.

VANESSA

(Greek)

Your resourcefulness will get you out of a dangerous situation.

VEDA

(Sanskrit)

A good friend wants to help you. Let her.

VERA

(Latin)

Shave your legs, curl your eyelashes, and apply some lipstick; your luck in love is about to change!

VERONA

(Italian)

When you least expect it, telling the truth instead of running from it will get you out of a jam.

VERONICA

(Latin), Veronique (French)

Anticipate a few more potholes before the road smoothes out.

VICTORIA

(Latin) Vicki, Vickie, Vicky, Vikki

A new friend will reinvigorate your dying social life.

VIDA

(Spanish)

An old flame pines for your love and affection. Do you believe in second chances?

VIOLET

(French) Violeta, Violetta

A friend needs your help.

VIRGINIA

(Latin)
Dry your tears. A broken love affair is for the best.

VITA

(Latin)
Your performance on an important project will earn you a promotion.

VIVIAN

(Latin) Viviana; Viveca (Scandinavian)
Your love life is about to heat up.

BOY NAMES

VALENTINO

(Italian)
Brace yourself for trouble in romance.

VAN

(Dutch)
A positive change in your attitude will bring someone new into your life.

VANCE

(English, Irish)

Great abundance and happiness is fated for you.

VARICK

(German)

A period of financial distress is in your future. Use your resources wisely.

VAUGHN

(Welsh)

You must make amends for a past wrong to truly move forward.

VERNON

(English)

Romantic success will bring you tremendous happiness and satisfaction.

VICENTE

(Spanish)

A wild adventure is on the horizon.

VICTOR

(Latin) Vic

Unexpected news that will forever change your future is on its way.

VIDAL

(Spanish)

The end of a love affair will take you by surprise.

VIGGO

(Scandinavian)

You will overcome an obstacle faster and more gracefully
than you expected.

VINCENT

(Latin) Vin, Vince, Vinnie, Vinny

Temporary relief from overwhelming responsibility will
allow you to catch your breath.

VITO

(Latin)

Overextending yourself will do nothing to forward
your success.

GIRL NAMES

WALKER

(English)

You have a loyal following of friends who will never
let you down.

WALLIS

(English)

Someone you wouldn't expect finds you irresistible.

WANDA

(German)

Learn to control your temper, or it will get you into trouble.

WAVERLY

(English)

You will cruise through life with relative ease.

WENDY

(Welsh) Wendi

A deep love will forever change your life.

WESLEY

(English) Weslie

Your smart, thoughtful choices will bring you
great success.

WHITLEY

(English)

Your sensitivity is a liability. Remember to keep things in perspective.

WHITNEY

(English)

Any jealous twinges are unfounded. Your lover is completely devoted to you.

WILLA

(German)

Strength and grace will see you through a difficult time.

WILLOW

(English)

Trust that a tough decision was the right one.

WINONA

(Lakota) Wynonna

Your overly emotional response to a problem will do nothing to get you closer to a resolution.

WREN

(English) Wrenn

Many social engagements lie ahead.

WYNNE

(Welsh) Wynn

Quick wit and intelligence will bring you much
career success.

BOY NAMES

WADE

(English)

Impulsivity and hasty decisions will bring an
unsatisfying result to an important project. Take your
time, be deliberate, and you can turn it around.

WAGNER

(German)

You will receive a significant return on your
recent investment.

WALKER

(English)

A short period of professional tribulations will be
overshadowed by a lasting romance.

WALLACE

(English)

You will overcome a professional obstacle that has
plagued you for too long.

WALTER

(German) Walt, Wally

Foolhardy romantic relationships will complicate your affairs.

WARNER

(English)

An adventurous journey will bring someone new into your life.

WARREN

(French)

An impulsive decision will actually turn out to be a good one. But don't make it a habit.

WAYLON

(English)

You will successfully complete a difficult project through hard work and painstaking attention to detail.

WAYNE

(English)

You will be recognized for a great achievement.

WEBB

(English)

Favorable business opportunities are at hand. Grab them!

WENDELL

(German)

Your personal and professional distress will be
short-lived.

WESLEY

(English) Wes

Use discretion and good sense in your encounters
with love.

WESTCOTT

(English) Wes

A romantic liaison will cause you fleeting
embarrassment, but it will soon pass.

WESTON

(English) Wes

Use your resources wisely. An unexpected expense will
drain your bank account.

WILLIAM

(English) Bill, Billy, Billie, Will, Willie, Wills; Willem (German)

After years of toil, lasting wealth will be yours.

WILSON

(English)

A comfortable and happy domestic life will usher you into
old age.

WINSTON

(English)

Don't let unfortunate news discourage you.
It's a minor setback.

WOLCOTT

(English)

You are destined for rapid advancement in your career.

WREN

(Welsh)

You will need to rework a course of action for it to end
in success.

WYATT

(English)

Misconstrued actions will get you into relationship
trouble. You will have some explaining to do.

WYCLEF

(English)

A new romance will be fleeting, but you'll enjoy the ride.

WYMAN

(English)

More effort and better planning are required to
accomplish a current goal.

GIRL NAMES

XAVIERA

(Arabic) Xavier

Anticipate a positive change of surroundings.

XENA

(Greek)

Your versatility sets you apart from the pack.

XIMENA

(Spanish)

When having doubts about a plan, get help before moving forward.

XIOMARA

(Teutonic)

Adjusting to a new environment will be difficult, but rest assured, you've made the right choice.

XUXA

(Portuguese)

Your hard work and diligence will soon be rewarded.

YADIRA

(Hebrew)

A happy family and moderate prosperity are in your future.

YAEL

(Hebrew)

The ease of a new relationship will pleasantly surprise you.

YAMINAH

(Arabic)

Hostility and anger will only further your problem.

YARELI

(American)

Your worries are for naught. Your plan of action is a good one.

YARITZA

(American)

A romance will end badly. Don't worry; he wasn't the one.

YASMIN

(Persian) Yasmeen, Yasmine, Yazmin

Your beauty will attract many suitors.

YEARDLY

(English)

Your career success is assured.

YESENIA

(Arabic) Yessenia

Slow down! You can't sustain your intensity without hurting yourself.

YOLANDA

(Greek)

A difficult year will teach you more than you realize.

YOSHI

(Japanese)

You are highly respected for your drive and attention to detail.

YURI

(Chinese)

You will never be in want of affection.

YVES

(French)

A pleasant but insignificant affair will be a nice reprieve from this otherwise stressful period.

YVETTE

(French)

When considering a questionable action, think twice.

YVONNE

(French)

Your athletic abilities and pursuits will bring you a type
of satisfaction that your career cannot.

ZADA

(Arabic)

You will be most fortunate in love.

ZADIE

(American), Zaidee (Arabic)

Your competition is nipping at your heels.
Pick up the pace!

ZAHARA

(Hebrew)

A new career will blossom.

ZAIDA

(Spanish)

You can't always be the peacemaker. Focus your energy
on yourself.

ZANE

(Scandinavian)

In your attitude and approach to life, you make a
bold statement.

ZARA

(Hebrew) Zaria

Your health will never cause you worry.

ZELDA

(German)

**Practicality and prudence will bring you moderate success.
For the big trophy, you're going to have to take a risk.**

ZENA

(Greek)

Your happiness lies in a return to spirituality.

ZERA

(Hebrew)

**The seed has been planted. Just wait, success will
undoubtedly sprout.**

ZOE

(Greek) Zoey, Zoie

**You are vibrant and vivacious. Your choices are not
always wise ones, but you certainly have enough fun.**

ZOLA

(French)

**A return to nature will bring you some much-
needed peace.**

BOY NAMES

XANDER

(Greek) Zander

A new romantic acquaintance will not have your best
interests at heart.

XAVIER

(Basque)

A resolution to a current problem will only come to pass if
you are willing to make a few necessary compromises.

YAHIR

(Hebrew) Yair

A personal issue will be more manageable than you
once thought.

YARDLEY

(English)

A risky investment will yield a surprising financial gain.

YASIR

(Arabic)

A hasty romance will negatively affect you and your future.

YOSEF

(Hebrew)

Luckily, an embarrassing social situation will
go unnoticed.

YULE

(English)
You will be profoundly lucky in love.

ZACHARIAH

(Hebrew) Zechariah
A significant return on your investments will allow you to take advantage of a promising opportunity.

ZACHARY

(Hebrew) Zachery, Zackary, Zackery, Zakary; Zack, Zach
Prosperity and good health are fated for you and your family.

ZAHIR

(Arabic) Zaire
You will make significant progress on a project but not without hard work.

ZANE

(English) Zain
A new someone will be completely enchanted by you.

ZAVIER

(Arabic)
An advantageous change will come disguised as an annoyance.

ZED

(Hebrew)

You are admired and will be recognized for your intellectual prowess.

ZEKE

(Hebrew)

Make sure you've got a backup plan. A friend's offer may not be sincere.

ZIGGY

(German)

Significant improvements in your romantic affairs will bring you great joy and relief from worry.

ZION

(Hebrew)

A romantic encounter with a mysterious stranger will forever change your life.

ZOLTAN

(Hungarian)

A solid return on an investment will ensure that there's excess cash in your pocket.

ZURI

(African)

A dramatic, life-changing experience will shock and delight you.

NUMEROLOGY

Use this ancient system to calculate the number that
corresponds with your name. Then use that number to learn
more about what your name says about your character.

1	2	3	4	5	6	7	8	9
A	B	C	D	E	F	G	H	I
J	K	L	M	N	O	P	Q	R
S	T	U	V	W	X	Y	Z	

1. List the letters of your name. Some people choose to use
   their first and last names. Some people choose to use their
   first, middle, and last names. Others choose to use a nick-
   name and their last name. It's up to you. Use the name to
   which you feel most connected.

   For example, *Pamela Edwards.*

2. Now list the corresponding numbers.

   Pamela   Edwards
   714531   5451941

3. Add the numbers together.

   7+1+4+5+3+1+5+4+5+1+9+4+1 = 50

4. If your number is 11, 22, or 33, stop here.

5. If not, add the individual numbers together.

   5+0=5

6. Your goal is to come up with a number between 1 and 9, or 11, 22, or 33. If your number is not 11, 22, or 33, and is beyond 9, add the individual numbers together again.

   This is your final number.

   Pamela's final number is 5.

THE NUMBERS BREAKDOWN

ONE

Independent, confident, egotistical, controlling,
demanding, dignified, loving.

TWO

Artistic, imaginative, romantic, intuitive, sensitive, peaceful,
emotional, private.

THREE

Lucky, ambitious, articulate, distracted, versatile, idealistic,
intellectual, optimistic.

FOUR

Dependable, faithful, stubborn, cautious, organized,
loyal, sensible.

FIVE

Overly analytical, critical, curious, smart, imaginative,
adventurous, restless, capricious.

SIX

Idealistic, devoted, social, refined, creative, sensitive,
self-righteous.

SEVEN

Spiritual, intuitive, introspective, detail-oriented, illusive, thoughtful.

EIGHT

Reserved, ambitious, tenacious, intense, goal-oriented, materialistic, needy.

NINE

Intelligent, brave, impulsive, impatient, generous, humanitarian.

The following master numbers are especially auspicious:

ELEVEN

Inspirational, intuitive, charismatic, articulate, visionary, artistic, inventive.

TWENTY-TWO

Powerful, magnetic, accomplished, advanced, intelligent, willful, nervous.

THIRTY-THREE

Influential, emotionally mature, altruistic, forgiving, nurturing, loving.

MOST POPULAR NAMES
OF PAST DECADES

2000s

Boys	Girls
1. Jacob	1. Emily
2. Michael	2. Madison
3. Joshua	3. Emma
4. Matthew	4. Hannah
5. Andrew	5. Abigail

1990s

Boys	Girls
1. Michael	1. Jessica
2. Christopher	2. Ashley
3. Matthew	3. Emily
4. Joshua	4. Sarah
5. Jacob	5. Samantha

1980s

Boys	Girls
1. Michael	1. Jessica
2. Christopher	2. Jennifer
3. Matthew	3. Amanda
4. Joshua	4. Ashley
5. David	5. Sarah

1970s

Boys	Girls
1. Michael	1. Jennifer
2. Christopher	2. Amy
3. Jason	3. Melissa
4. David	4. Michelle
5. James	5. Kimberly

1960s

Boys	Girls
1. Michael	1. Lisa
2. David	2. Mary
3. John	3. Susan
4. James	4. Karen
5. Robert	5. Kimberly

1950s

Boys	Girls
1. James	1. Mary
2. Michael	2. Linda
3. Robert	3. Patricia
4. John	4. Susan
5. David	5. Deborah

1940s

Boys	Girls
1. James	1. Mary
2. Robert	2. Linda
3. John	3. Barbara
4. William	4. Patricia
5. Richard	5. Carol

1930s

Boys	Girls
1. Robert	1. Mary
2. James	2. Betty
3. John	3. Barbara
4. William	4. Shirley
5. Richard	5. Patricia

1920s

Boys	Girls
1. Robert	1. Mary
2. John	2. Dorothy
3. James	3. Helen
4. William	4. Betty
5. Charles	5. Margaret

1910s

Boys	Girls
1. John	1. Mary
2. William	2. Helen
3. James	3. Dorothy
4. Robert	4. Margaret
5. Joseph	5. Ruth

1900s

Boys	Girls
1. John	1. Mary
2. William	2. Helen
3. James	3. Margaret
4. George	4. Anna
5. Charles	5. Ruth

1890s

Boys	Girls
1. John	1. Mary
2. William	2. Anna
3. James	3. Margaret
4. George	4. Helen
5. Charles	5. Elizabeth

Text © 2008 Chronicle Books LLC
Illustrations © 2008 Jennifer Sly

Library of Congress Cataloging-in-Publication Data available.

ISBN: 978-0-8118-6381-0
Manufactured in China

10 9 8 7 6 5 4 3 2 1

Chronicle Books LLC
680 Second Street
San Francisco, CA 94107
www.chroniclebooks.com